Thomas J. Murrey

Fifty soups

Thomas J. Murrey

Fifty soups

ISBN/EAN: 9783742832016

Manufactured in Europe, USA, Canada, Australia, Japa

Cover: Foto ©Gila Hanssen / pixelio.de

Manufactured and distributed by brebook publishing software
(www.brebook.com)

Thomas J. Murrey

Fifty soups

BY

THOMAS J. MURREY,

*Formerly professional caterer of the Continental Hotel, Phil-
adelphia, Astor House, New York, and other leading
hotels. Author of "Salads and Sauces,"
"Valuable Cooking Recipes," etc.*

NEW YORK

WHITE, STOKES, & ALLEN

1884

CONTENTS.

REMARKS ON SOUPS.

Soups, like salads, present an excellent opportunity for the cook to display good taste and judgment.

The great difficulty lies in selecting the most appropriate soup for each particular occasion ; it would be well to first select your bill of fare, after which decide upon the soup.

The season, and force of circumstances, may compel you to decide upon a heavy fish, such as salmon, trout, or other oleaginous fishes, and heavy joints and entrées.

Under these circumstances it must necessarily follow that a light soup should begin the dinner, and *vice versa ;* for large parties, one light and one heavy soup is always in order.

There is as much art in arranging a bill of fare and harmonizing the peculiarities of the various dishes, as there is in preparing the colors for a painting ; the soup represents the pivot upon which harmony depends.

Soups may be divided into four classes: clear, thick, purées or bisques, and chowders. A puree is made by rubbing the cooked ingredi‹ ents through a fine sieve; an ordinary thick soup is made by adding various thickening in‹ gredients to the soup stock; clear soups are, properly speaking, the juices of meats, served in a convenient and appetizing form.

Chowders are quite distinct from the fore‹ going, being compounds of an infinite variety of fish, flesh, fowl, or vegetables, in proportions to suit the fluctuating ideas of the cook; the object sought is to prepare a thick, highly seasoned compound, without reducing the in‹ gredients to the consistency of a purée.

Soup Stock.—The word stock when used in cooking means the foundation or basis upon which soups and sauces depend ; it is therefore the most important part of soup making. Care should be excercised that nothing in the least tainted or decayed enters the stock pot ; it is very desirable that soup stock be prepared a day or two before it is wanted ; the season‹ ing should be added in moderation at first, as it is difficult to restore a soup that has been damaged by over seasoning.

Milk or cream should be boiled and strained,

and added hot when intended for soups ; when eggs are used beat them thoroughly, and add while the soup is hot. Should they be added when the soup is boiling, they are very apt to separate, and give the soup the appearance of having curdled ; the best plan is to beat up the egg with a little of the warm soup, then add it to the soup gradually.

In summer, soup stock should be boiled from day to day, if kept any length of time, else it may become sour : should this happen, add a piece of charcoal to the soup, boil, cool, and strain into freshly scalded earthen or porclain-lined ware. On no account allow the soup stock to become cold in an iron pot or saucepan.

To make Beef Stock.—Take six pounds of soup meat, cut it up into good sized pieces, break the bones into small pieces, place them in the stock pot, and add five quarts of cold water and two ounces of salt ; boil slowly for five hours, remove the scum as fast as it rises ; cut up three white turnips and three carrots, add these to the soup with two stalks of celery, one large onion quartered, six cloves, teaspoonful of whole peppers, and a small bunch of herbs.

When the vegetables are thoroughly cooked, strain the soup into a large saucepan, and set it on back of range to keep hot, but not to boil, cut one pound of lean raw beef into fine pieces, put in into a saucepan, and add the whites and shells of four eggs ; season with salt, pepper, and a little chopped parsley or celery tops ; squeeze these together with your hand for fifteen minutes, until they are thoroughly incorporated, then add to the warm soup ; allow the soup to simmer slowly one hour ; taste for seasoning ; strain into crocks, or serve. This is now called consommé or bouillon, and is the basis of nearly all soups ; such items as macaroni, sago, Italian paste, Macedoine, and, in fact, nearly all kinds of cereals and soup ingredients may be added to this stock at different times to produce variety ; they should all be boiled separately before adding to the soup.

Calf's feet and knuckle of veal may be added to the original or first pot if a very strong stock is required.

Veal Stock.—Chop up three slices of bacon and two pounds of the neck of veal ; place in a stewpan with a pint of water or beef stock, and simmer for half an hour ; then add two quarts of stock, one onion, a carrot, a bouquet of herbs, four stalks of celery, half a teaspoonful of bruised whole peppers, and a pinch of nutmeg with a teaspoonful of salt ; boil gently for two hours, removing the scum in the meantime. Strain into an earthen crock, and when cold remove the fat. A few bones of poultry added, with an additional quantity of water or stock, will improve it.

Croutons, or fried bread crumbs for soups, are prepared in this way :—Cut slices of stale home-made bread half an inch thick, trim off all crust and cut each slice into squares ; fry these in very hot fat; drain them on a clean napkin, and add six or eight to each portion of soup.

Marrow Dumplings for Soups.—Grate the crust of a breakfast roll, and break the remainder into crumbs ; soak these in cold milk ; drain, and add two ounces of flour ; chop up half a pound of beef marrow freed from skin and sinews ; beat up the yolks of five eggs ; mix all together thoroughly, if too moist add some of the grated crumbs ; salt and pepper to taste ; form into small round dumplings ; boil them in the soup for half an hour before serving.

Glaze.—Glaze is made from rich soup stock, boiled down until it forms a dark, strong jelly. It is used in coloring soups and sauces and for glazing entrées. It should be kept in a stone crock.

Artichoke Soup.—Melt a piece of butter the size of an egg in a saucepan ; then fry in it one white turnip sliced, one red onion sliced, three pounds of Jerusalem artichokes washed, pared, and sliced, and a rasher of bacon. Stir these in the boiling butter for about ten minutes, add gradually one pint of stock. Let all boil together until the vegetables are thoroughly cooked, then add three pints more of stock ; stir it well ; add pepper and salt to taste, strain and press the vegetables through a sieve, and add one pint of boiling milk. Boil for five minutes more and serve.

Asparagus Soup.—Take seventy-five heads of asparagus ; cut away the hard, tough part, and boil the rest until tender. Drain them, and throw half into cold water until the soup is nearly ready, and press the other half through a hair sieve. Stir the pressed asparagus into two pints of stock, and let it boil ; add salt, pepper, and a small lump of sugar. Cut the remaining heads of asparagus into peas ; put them into the soup, and in a few minutes serve. If necessary color with a little spinach green.

Barley Soup.—Put into a stock pot a knuckle of veal and two pounds of shoulder of mutton chopped up ; cover with one gallon of cold water ; season with salt, whole peppers, and a blade of mace ; boil for three hours, removing the scum as fast as it rises. Wash half a pint of barley in cold water, drain and cover it with milk, and let it stand for half an hour, drain and add to the soup ; boil half an hour longer, moderately ; strain, trim the meat from the bone, chop up a little parsley or celery tops, add a tablespoonful to the soup and serve.

Beef Tea.—Take half a pound of lean beef ; cut it up into small bits ; let it soak in a pint of water for three-quarters of an hour; then put both into a quart champagne bottle with just a suspicion of salt. Cork tightly, and wire the cork, so as to prevent its popping out. Set the bottle in a saucepan full of warm water, boil gently for an hour and a half, and strain through a napkin. Beef tea, without the fibrine of the meat, if administered often to a patient, will tend to weaken, instead of strengthening the invalid ; always add about a teaspoonful of finely chopped raw meat to a goblet of the tea, and let it stand in the tea for about five minutes before serving.

Bisque of Crabs.—Boil twelve hard-shell crabs for thirty minutes, and drain ; when cold break them apart, pick out the meat carefully, scrape off all fat adhering to the upper shell, and save these for deviled crabs (an excellent recipe for deviled crabs may be found in " Salads and Sauces.")

Set the crab meat aside ; put the under shell and the claws in a mortar with half a pound of butter and a cupful of cold boiled rice, and pound them as smooth as possible ; then put this into a saucepan, and add a heaping tea-spoonful of salt, a bouquet of assorted herbs, a dozen whole peppers, a blade of mace, and three quarts of stock ; boil slowly for one hour, pour it through a sieve, and work as much of the pulp through the sieve as possible. Place the soup on the range to keep warm, but not to boil.

Beat up the yolk of one egg, and add it slowly to a quart of warm milk previously boil-ed ; whisk the milk into the soup ; taste for seasoning. Now take the crab meat and heat it in a little boiling water, drain, put it into a hot soup tureen, pour the soup over it and serve.

Bisque of Lobster.—Procure two large live lobsters ; chop them up while raw, shells and all ; put them into a mortar with three-fourths of a pound of butter, three raw eggs, and one quarter of a pound of cold boiled rice : pound to a paste, moisten with a little water or stock, then set aside. Fry out two slices of bacon fat, add to it one minced onion, a tablespoonful of chopped celery tops, one chopped long red pepper, one sliced carrot, and a quart of stock, boil and pour the whole into a saucepan. Add the lobster and three pints more of stock ; boil slowly for two hours ; strain, and rub the ingredients through a sieve. Return to the soup ; keep it warm, but do not allow it to boil. If too thick, add a little more stock ; add salt to taste. Boil one quart of cream ; whisk it into the soup ; taste again for seasoning ; pour it into a hot soup tureen, and send to table.

This soup can be prepared by following receipt for bisque of crab, or it may be prepared by adding boiled lobster to a strong veal stock, and colored red by pounding the coral with butter, and adding this to the soup.

Bouille-abaisse.—Take six pounds of codfish ; cut it up into small pieces ; chop two red onions ; put them in a stewpan with an ounce of butter ; let them brown without burning. Now add the fish and four tablespoonfuls of fine olive-oil, a bruised clove of garlic, two bay leaves, four slices of lemon peeled and quartered, half a pint of Shrewsbury tomato catsup, and half a salt-spoonful of saffron. Add sufficient hot soup stock to cover the whole ; boil slowly for half to three-quarters of an hour ; skim carefully while boiling ; when ready to serve add a tablespoonful of chopped celery tops.

Cauliflower Soup.—Fry half an onion in a very little butter ; when it is a light brown add a tablespoonful of minced raw ham and two or three stalks of celery, then add a quart of soup stock ; simmer slowly for half an hour. Boil for twenty-five or thirty minutes one medium-sized head of cauliflower in water slightly salted. Strain the contents of the frying-pan into a saucepan, and add one quart more of stock. Drain the cauliflower ; rub it throngh a fine sieve into the stock ; boil just once ; draw to one side of the fire ; taste for seasoning. Now dissolve a teaspoonful of rice flour in half a cupful of cold milk ; whisk the soup thoroughly ; pour into a hot tureen, and serve.

Chestnut Soup.—Remove the outer peel or coating from twenty-five Italian chestnuts ; pour scalding water over them, and rub off the inner coating. Put them into a saucepan with one quart of soup stock, and boil for three-quarters of an hours ; drain ; rub them through a colander, then through a sieve, with one tablespoonful of cracker dust, or pound to a paste in a mortar ; season with salt and pepper; add gradually the stock in which they were boiled; add one pint more of stock; boil once, and draw to one side of the fire.

Beat up the yolks of two raw eggs; add them to one quart of warm milk; whisk the milk into the soup; taste for seasoning; pour into a hot tureen, and send to table with croutons.

Chicken Broth for the Invalid.—Procure a dry-picked Philadelphia roasting chicken; cut it in halves; put one half in the ice box; chop the other half into neat pieces; put it into a small saucepan; add one quart of cold water, a little salt and a leaf of celery; simmer gently for two hours; remove the oily particles thoroughly; strain the broth into a bowl; when cooled a little, serve to the convalescent. Serve the meat with the broth.

Chicken Soup.—Take three young male chickens; cut them up; put them in a saucepan with three quarts of veal stock. (A sliced carrot, one turnip, and one head of celery may be put with them and removed before the soup is thickened.) Let them simmer for an hour. Remove all the white flesh; return the rest of the birds to the soup, and boil gently for two hours. Pour a little of the liquid over a quarter of a pound of bread crumbs, and when they are well soaked put it in a mortar with the white flesh of the birds, and pound the whole to a smooth paste : add a pinch of ground mace, salt, and a little cayenne pepper ; press the mixture through a sieve, and boil once more, adding a pint of boiling cream : thicken with a little flour mixed in cold milk ; remove the bones, and serve.

Chicken Soup, No. 2.—Cut up one chicken, put into a stewpan two quarts of cold water, a teaspoonful of salt, and one pod of red pepper ; when half done add two desert spoonfuls of well washed rice : when thoroughly cooked, remove the bird from the soup, tear a part of the breast into shreds (saving the remainder of the fowl for a salad), and add it to the soup with a wine-glass full of cream.

Clam Broth.—Procure three dozen little-neck clams in the shell ; wash them well in cold water ; put them in a saucepan, cover with a quart of hot water ; boil fifteen minutes ; drain ; remove the shells ; chop up the clams, and add them to the hot broth with a pat of butter; salt if necessary and add a little cayenne ; boil ten minutes, pour into a soup tureen, add a slice of toast, and send to table. This is the mode adopted when we do not have a clam opener in the house.

Raw, freshly opened clams should be chopped fine and prepared in the manner above described. The large clams are better for chowders than for stews and broth.

Clam Chowder.—Chop up fifty large clams; cut eight medium-sized potatoes into small square pieces, and keep them in cold water until wanted.

Chop one large, red onion fine, and cut up half a pound of larding pork into small pieces.

Procure an iron pot, and see that it is very clean and free from rust; set it on the range, and when very hot, throw the pieces of pork into it, fry them brown; next add the onion, and fry it brown; add one fourth of the chopped clams, then one fourth of the chopped potato, and two pilot crackers quartered, a teaspoonful of salt, one chopped, long, red pepper, a teaspoonful of powdered thyme and half a pint of canned tomato pulp. Repeat this process until the clams and potato are used, omitting the seasoning; add hot water enough to cover all, simmer slowly three hours. Should it become too thick, add more hot water; occasionally remove the pot from the range, take hold of the handle, and twist the pot round several times; this is done to prevent the chowder from burning. On no account disturb the

20

chowder with a spoon or ladle until done ; now taste for seasoning, as it is much easier to season properly after the chowder is cooked than before. A few celery tops may be added if desired.

Consommé.—This is nothing more than beef stock, with a little more attention given to clarifying it. It is always acceptable if the dinner to follow is composed of heavy joints and side dishes. If the party consists of more than twenty, serve one thick soup and one light soup or consommé.

Consommé Colbert.—Prepare a strong consommé ; add to two quarts of it a tablespoonful each of shredded young turnips and carrots and a tablespoonful of green peas ; simmer until the vegetables are tender ; taste for seasoning.

Poach four eggs in hot water in the usual manner ; send these to table with the soup. In serving add one poached egg to each plate. It is well always to poach two extra eggs to be used should any of the others be broken in the service.

Cream of Celery.—Cut up six stalks of celery into half-inch pieces ; put them into a saucepan with one red onion quartered, one blade of mace, salt, and a few whole peppers ;

add a quart of veal stock, and boil for one hour. Rub the ingredients through a sieve ; put the pulp into a saucepan, and add one quart more of veal stock ; boil ; then draw to one side of fire to keep hot.

Boil three pints of cream ; strain it into the soup ; whisk the soup at the same time (if not thick enough to suit your taste add a little flour) ; taste for seasoning ; pour it into a hot tureen ; serve with small pieces of toast or croutons.

Cream of Rice.—Wash thoroughly a half pound of rice ; pick out all imperfect or colored grains ; put it into a saucepan and add two quarts of stock. Boil slowly for one hour ; then rub the rice through a sieve twice ; return it to the stock ; season with salt and pepper. Care must be exercised that the rice does not adhere to the bottom of the saucepan. Simmer until wanted. Beat up the yolks of two eggs ; add them slowly to a quart of warm milk previously boiled ; whisk the milk into the soup, which must not be very hot ; then pour it into a hot tureen, and serve.

Cream Soup.—Prepare two quarts of strong veal stock ; set it on the back part of the range to simmer.

Boil one quart of cream ; whisk it into the

stock; pour it into a hot tureen, and serve with croutons. If convenient the breast of a boiled chicken may be added.

Fish Chowder.—Take two fine, fresh codfish, weighing six pounds each; clean them well; cut the fish lengthwise from the bone, and cut it into pieces two inches square. Chop up the bones and heads; put them into a saucepan; add three quarts of warm water, one red onion sliced, heaping teaspoonful of salt, a dozen bruised peppercorns, and a few stalks of celery. Boil until the fish drops from the bones; then strain into another saucepan.

Cut into small squares one peck of small potatoes and a pound and a half of salt pork; arrange the fish, pork, and potatoes into mounds; divide each equally into four parts; add one quarter of the fish to the stock, next a quarter of the pork, then a quarter of the potato, and three pilot crackers, broken into quarters, salt, pepper, and a little thyme. Repeat this process until the remaining three quarters of pork, fish, and potato, are used; cover all with warm milk; simmer slowly until the fish is tender, care being taken that the soup does not boil over; now taste for seasoning, serve as neatly as possible.

The above is the old-fashioned New England fish chowder. Clams may be used instead of fish.

German Soup.—Melt half an ounce of fresh butter in a sauce-pan ; when very hot, add half an onion, chopped fine, and a teas‧poonful of caraway seeds. When the onion is slightly browned, add three quarts of strong veal stock, well seasoned ; simmer gently for three quarters of an hour. Prepare some mar‧row dumplings ; boil them in water, or a por‧tion of the soup, and serve.

Giblet Soup.—An economical, and at the same time excellent, soup, is made from the legs, neck, heart, wings, and gizzard of all kinds of poultry. These odds and ends are usually plentiful about the holidays.

To turn them to account, follow general in‧structions for chicken soup ; add a little rice, and your soup is complete.

Green Turtle Soup.—Many housewives im‧agine that green turtle is too expensive, and too difficult to prepare for household use, and for these reasons it is seldom met with in pri‧vate families, except in tin cans. Even this is not always made from turtle.

This soup is not any more expensive than many other kinds. A small turtle may be pur‧chased at Fulton market for from ten to twenty cents per pound, and weighing from fifteen to forty pounds, the price varying according to the law of supply and demand. The only objection to small turtles is that they do not contain a very large percentage of the green fat, so highly prized by epicures.

Procure a live turtle, cut off the head, and allow it to drain and cool over night; next morning place it on the working table, lay it on its back, and make an incision round the inner edge of the shell; then remove it. Now remove the intestines carefully, and be very careful that you do not break the gall; throw these away; cut off the fins and all fleshy particles, and set them aside; trim out the fat, which has a blueish tint when raw; wash it well in several waters. Chop up the upper and under shells with a cleaver; put them with the fins into a large saucepan; cover them with boiling water; let stand ten minutes; drain and rub off the horny, scaly particles, with a kitchen towel.

Scald a large saucepan, and put all the meat and shell into it (except the fat); cover with hot water; add a little salt, and boil four hours. Skim carefully, and drain; put the meat into a large crock; remove the bones, and boil the fat in the stock. This does not take very long if first scalded. When done, add it also to the crock; pour the stock into another crock; let it cool, and remove all scum and oily particles; this is quite work enough for one day. Clean the saucepans used, and dry them thoroughly.

Next day fry out half a pound of fat ham; then add one chopped onion, one bay leaf, six cloves, one blade of mace, two tablespoonfuls of chopped celery tops, a tablespoonful of salt, a teaspoonful of white pepper, and one quart of ordinary soup stock. Simmer for half an hour. Now put the turtle stock on the fire; when hot strain the seasoning into it; remove the turtle from the other crock, cut it up, and add to the stock; now add a pint of dry sherry.

Do not let the soup come to a boil; taste for seasoning, and if herbs are needed tie a string to a bunch of mixed herbs, throw them into the soup, and tie the other end to the saucepan handle; taste often, and when palatable, remove the herbs. If the soup is not dark enough, brown a very little flour and add to it. Keep the soup quite hot until served; add quartered slices of lemon and the yolk of a hard boiled egg, quartered just before serving; send to table with a decanter of sherry.

The yolks of the eggs may be worked to a

paste, and made into round balls to imitate turtle eggs if this is desired.

I have placed before my readers this complicated receipt in as simple a form as it is possible to do, having carefully avoided all the technical formulas used in the profession.

Gumbo Soup.—Cut up two chickens, two slices of ham, and two onions into dice ; flour them, and fry the whole to a light brown ; then fill the frying pan with boiling water ; stir it a few minutes, and turn the whole into a saucepan containing three quarts of boiling water.   Let it boil for forty minutes, removing the scum.

In the meantime soak three pints of ochra in cold water for twenty minutes ; cut them into thin slices, and add to the other ingredients ; let it boil for one hour and a half.   Add a quart of canned tomatoes and a cupful of boiled rice half an hour before serving.

Julienne Soup.—Cut into fine shreds, an inch long, two carrots, two turnips, two heads of celery, and the white ends of two spring leeks.   Put them into a frying pan, with one ounce of butter, a teaspoonful of salt, and one lump of cut sugar ; simmer until tender, then add a cupful of stock.   Put two quarts of veal stock in a saucepan ; add the vegetables, and a teaspoonful of chopped parsley, a little fresh sorrel if convenient (wild wood sorrel is the best for julienne) shredded. Taste for seasoning ; boil once, and serve.

Lentil Soup.—Lentils are very nutritious, and form the basis of a most excellent soup ; but they are little used in American cookery. Soak a pint of dry lentils for two hours ; put them in a saucepan ; add two quarts of cold water, half an onion, two or three celery tops, salt, whole peppers, and two or three ounces of the small end of a ham. Boil gently for three hours ; add a little more hot water, if the quantity has been reduced by boiling, pour through a sieve, remove the ham, onion and celery ; rub the lentils through a sieve, return to the soup; whisk it thoroughly; taste for seasoning, and serve with croutons.

Liebig's Soup.—An excellent soup may be prepared at short notice, as follows:—Take half an onion, three or four outer stocks of celery, one carrot sliced, salt, pepper, and a very little mace. Boil these in two quarts of water for half an hour ; strain, and add to the water two table-spoonfuls of Liebig's Extract of meat ; whisk thoroughly, taste for seasoning, and serve.

Macaroni Soup.—Boil half a pound of

Macaroni for half an hour, in three pints of water slightly salted; add a blade of mace. When done, drain, and cut it into two inch pieces. Put three pints of soup stock into a saucepan; add the macaroni; taste for seasoning, boil a moment and serve.

Mock Turtle Soup.—Take half a calf's head, with the skin on; remove the brains. Wash the head in several waters, and let it soak in cold water for an hour. Put it in a saucepan with five quarts of beef stock; let it simmer gently for an hour; remove the scum carefully. Take up the head and let it get cold; cut the meat from the bones into pieces an inch square, and set them in the ice-box.

Dissolve two ounces of butter in a frying pan; mince a large onion, and fry it in the butter until nicely browned, and add to the stock in which the head was cooked. Return the bones to the stock; simmer the soup, removing the scum until no more rises. Put in a carrot, a turnip, a bunch of parsley, a bouquet of herbs, a dozen outer stalks of celery, two blades of mace and the rind of one lemon, grated; salt and pepper to taste. Boil gently for two hours, and strain the soup through a cloth. Mix three ounces of browned flour with a pint of the soup; let simmer until it thickens, then add it to the soup. Take the pieces of head out of the ice-box, and add to the soup; let them simmer until quite tender. "Before serving add a little Worcestershire sauce, a tablespoonful of anchovy paste, a gobletful of port or sherry, and two lemons sliced, each slice quartered, with the rind trimmed off." Warm the wine a very little before adding it to the soup. Keep in ice-box three or four days before using. Serve the brains as a side dish.

Mulligatawny Soup.—Divide a large chicken into neat pieces; take a knuckle of veal, and chop it up; put all into a large saucepan, and add one gallon of water; salt; boil for three hours or until reduced one-third. Put an ounce of butter in a hot frying pan, cut up two red onions, and fry them in the butter. Into a half pint of the stock put two heaping tablespoonfuls of curry powder; add this to the onion, then add the whole to the soup, now taste for seasoning. Some like a little wine, but these are the exception and not the rule. Before serving add half a slice of lemon to each portion. Many prefer a quantity of rice to be added to the soup before it is finished; the rice should be first well washed and parboiled.

Mutton Broth.—Take four pounds of lean mutton trimmings; cut them into neat pieces;

put them into a saucepan ; add three quarts of cold water, one heaping teaspoonful of salt. Bruise, and add six peppercorns, three or four celery tops, and one young leek. Boil slowly.for two hours; remove the scum as it rises. Boil a cupful of rice for twenty minutes ; add it to the soup, and taste for seasoning ; remove the celery, leek, and mutton bones ; pour the soup into a hot tureen, and serve.

Substitute a knuckle of veal for mutton, and you will have an excellent veal broth.

Onion Soup.—Peel and cut into small pieces three medium-sized onions ; fry them in a little butter until tender, but not brown ; pour over them a pint of stock ; add a little salt and cayenne. Simmer for fifteen minutes ; press the soup through a sieve ; put it in a saucepan, and add three tablespoonfuls of grated bread crumbs, and half a gobletful of hot cream. Taste for seasoning, and serve with small slices of toast.

Oxtail Soup.—Take two oxtails ; cut them into joints, and cut each joint into four pieces ; put them into a pan with two ounces of butter, and fry them for ten minutes. Slice two onions, one turnip, two carrots, and a dozen outer stalks of celery, and fry in the same butter, with three slices of bacon cut up fine ; fry to a light brown. Turn the ingredients into a saucepan with a quart of stock or ham water, and boil quickly for half an hour, then add two more quarts of stock, a bouquet of herbs, two bay-leaves, a dozen whole peppers crushed, a few cloves, and salt to taste. Simmer until the meat is quite tender; then take it out; strain the soup; skim off the fat, and thicken with two ounces of flour. Return the meat to the soup; add a tablespoonful of Worcestershire, and a cupful of sherry, and serve with grated rusks.

Oyster Soup.—Wet a saucepan with cold water; pour into it two quarts of milk. When at boiling point, add two dozen oysters and a pint of oyster liquor well seasoned with salt and pepper. Dissolve a tablespoonful of rice flour in a little cold milk; finally add a large tablespoonful of table butter; do not let the soup boil again as it will contract the oysters. Pour into a tureen, taste for salting, and serve, a few broken crackers may be added. The object in wetting the pan is to prevent the milk from burning.

Pea Soup.—Cut two large slices of ham into dice, with a sliced onion, and fry them in a little bacon fat until they are lightly browned. Cut up one turnip, one large carrot, four outer stalks of celery, and one leek into small pieces ; add these last ingredients to the ham and onion, and let them simmer for fifteen minutes ; then pour over them three quarts of corned-beef water or hot water, and add a pint of split peas which have been soaked in cold water over night.

Boil gently until the peas are quite tender stirring constantly to prevent burning ; then add salt and pepper to taste, and a teaspoonful of brown sugar. Remove the soup from the fire, and rub through a sieve ; if it is not thick enough to suit your taste, add a few ounces of flour mixed smoothly in a little cold milk ; return the soup to the fire, and simmer for half an hour. Cut up four slices of American bread into small dice, and fry the pieces in very hot fat until nicely browned ; place them on a napkin or towel, and add a few to each plate or tureen of soup just before it goes to table.

Pea Soup, Economical.—Boil for four hours two quarts of green pea hulls in four quarts of water, in which beef, mutton, or fowl has been boiled, then add a bunch or bouquet of herbs, salt and pepper, a teaspoonful of butter, and a quart of milk. Rub through a hair sieve, thicken with a little flour, and serve with croutons, as in the foregoing receipt.

Potato Soup.—Wash and peel two dozen small sized potatoes ; put them into a saucepan with two onions ; add three quarts of corned-beef water ; boil for one hour and a half until the potatoes fall to pieces. Pour the soup through a sieve, and rub the potato through it to a fine pulp ; put the whole into the saucepan again ; when very hot add a pint of hot rich cream, salt and pepper, if necessary ; whisk thoroughly ; pour into a tureen, add croutons, and serve.

Purée of Beans.—Soak two quarts of small, white beans over night ; change the water twice ; drain, put them into a pot or saucepan, and cover them with cold water. Boil slowly for six hours ; as the water evaporates, add hot water. One hour before the beans are cooked add one pound of salt pork, a bunch of fresh herbs, half a dozen whole cloves, salt if necessary ; when done pour the soup through a sieve, remove the pork and seasoning, and rub the soup through a sieve ; add the pulp to the stock ; taste for seasoning ; pour the soup into a tureen, add croutons and serve. Many prefer a ham bone to pork.

Purée of Clams.—Chop twenty-five large hard-shell clams, very fine, and put them aside ; fry half a chopped red onion in an ounce of hot butter; add a teaspoonful of chopped celery tops, a blade of mace, one salted anchovy, six whole peppers, and a pint of soup stock. Let it boil; then strain into a saucepan; add the chopped clams and one quart of stock or hot water. Boil slowly one hour; strain all the clams through a sieve twice, and return to the stock; season with salt and cayenne. Keep the soup warm, but do not let it boil again; taste for seasoning. Boil one pint of cream in a saucepan previously wet with cold water; strain it, and add to the soup slowly. Mix a teaspoonful of rice flour in a little cold milk; add to the soup; whisk the soup; taste again for seasoning; pour it into a hot tureen, and serve.

Rabbit Soup.—Cut up two jack rabbits into neat pieces; put them into a stewpan containing one quarter of a pound of melted butter; add a slice of fat bacon cut into small pieces. Fry for five minutes in the butter; slice two small carrots, and two red onions, and add to the saucepan with one bay leaf, one blade of mace, four cloves, a few green celery stalks, one ounce of salt, and one long red pepper.

Pour over all, one gallon of stock; simmer gently for nearly three hours; skim carefully;

strain into a saucepan, and set on back of range to keep hot, but not to boil. Add half a pint of dry sherry, and serve with croutons. If not dark enough add a little glaze.

Scotch Broth.—Take two pounds of mutton trimmings; cut into neat pieces; put into a saucepan with three quarts of water, one large red onion, salt, and a dozen whole peppers. Boil gently, and remove the scum as it rises; wash half a pint of barley; soak it while the soup is boiling, and add it at the end of the first hour. Let the soup boil for two hours longer; taste for seasoning; pour slowly into a soup tureen, leaving the meat in the saucepan. Some prefer to take the meat out of the soup, and after removing the bones they return the meat to the soup.

Sorrel Soup.—Sorrel is an excellent ingredient for soup. Its acid leaves are much appreciated by the French; the wild sorrel may be used, but now that truck gardeners are cultivating it extensively, it will be found less troublesome to use the latter.

The Germans make the best sorrel soup; their recipe is as follows:—Wash and pick over two quarts of sorrel; remove the stems; then cut the sorrel into pieces. Heat two ounces of butter in a small saucepan; add the sorrel and a few blades of chives ; cover without water and allow it to steam for half an hour. Stir to prevent burning ; sprinkle over this a tablespoonful of flour free from lumps. Now add three quarts of well-seasoned veal stock ; taste for seasoning ; boil once, and send to table with croutons or small bits of toast. This an excellent spring and summer soup.

Spring Soup.—Take two quarts of nicely seasoned veal stock ; place it on the range to keep hot, but not to boil. Cut into neat strips four young carrots, four young spring turnips, and two spring leeks ; add them to the stock. Now add half a pint of fresh green peas ; boil gently for fifteen minutes ; taste for seasoning, and serve.

Tomato Soup.—Cut four ounces of ham into dice ; slice two onions, and fry with ham in two ounces of butter ; when browned turn them into a saucepan containing three quarts of stock or corned-beef water, and add three carrots, two turnips, and one long red pepper, and a dozen outer stalks of celery. Simmer gently for one hour ; then add a quart of canned tomatoes ; boil gently for another hour ; rub the whole through a sieve, and simmer again with the liquor a few minutes ; add salt, and serve with fried bread crumbs.

Turkey Soup.—Take the remains of a cold roast turkey, trim off all the meat, break up the bones, and put them into a saucepan ; cover them with two quarts of veal stock ; salt and cayenne to taste. Boil gently for one hour ; strain and skim. Now add the flesh of the turkey ; simmer gently ; dissolve a table-spoonful of rice flour in a little cold milk, and add it to the soup. Let it come to a boil ; taste for seasoning, and serve with croutons.

Vegetable Soup.—Wash and clean two carrots and two turnips ; cut them into slices, and cut each slice into small narrow strips ; put them into a saucepan with four stalks of celery cut into inch pieces, a dozen button onions, one long red pepper, and a teaspoon-ful of salt ; add three quarts of soup stock ; boil until the vegetables are tender, add a lump of sugar, and serve. The carrots and turnips may be cut into fancy shapes with a vegetable cutter.

Vermicelli Soup.—Take one quarter of a pound of vermicelli ; break it into pieces, and boil it for five minutes ; drain and add it to three pints of strong soup stock. Boil once ; draw to one side, and simmer gently for twenty min-utes. Should any scum arise, remove it ; taste for seasoning, and send to table with a little Parmesan cheese.

www.ingramcontent.com/pod-product-compliance
Lightning Source LLC
Chambersburg PA
CBHW032143080426
42733CB00008B/1182